UNDERSTANDING
JUDAISM

ORIGINS BELIEFS PRACTICES HOLY TEXTS SACRED PLACES

UNDERSTANDING
JUDAISM

ORIGINS BELIEFS PRACTICES HOLY TEXTS SACRED PLACES

CARL S. EHRLICH

WATKINS PUBLISHING
LONDON

In fond memory of Judith "Cousin Judy" Mastai (1945–2001)

Understanding Judaism
Carl S. Ehrlich

This edition first published in the United Kingdom and Ireland in 2010 by
Watkins Publishing, an imprint of Duncan Baird Publishers
Sixth Floor, Castle House, 75–76 Wells Street, London, W1T 3QH

Conceived, created and designed by Duncan Baird Publishers

British Library Cataloguing-in-Publication Data:
A CIP record for this book is available from the British Library

Library of Congress Cataloging-in-Publication Data

Ehrlich, Carl S.
  Understanding Judaism : origins, beliefs, practices, holy texts, sacred places / Carl S. Ehrlich.
-- 1st paperback ed.
    p. cm.
  Includes bibliographical references and index.
  ISBN 978-1-907486-17-3 (alk. paper)
  1. Judaism. 2. Judaism--History. 3. Jews--History. I. Title.
  BM562.E43 2010
  296--dc22
                                    2010002379

ISBN: 978-1-907486-17-3

10 9 8 7 6 5 4 3 2 1

Typeset in Garamond Three
Colour reproduction by Scanhouse, Malaysia
Printed and bound in Thailand by Imago

NOTES
The abbreviations BCE and CE are used throughout this book:
BCE Before the Common Era (the equivalent of BC)
CE Common Era (the equivalent of AD)

Page 2: Two ultra-Orthodox men praying at the Western Wall in Jerusalem, Judaism's holiest site
(see pp.68–9).

Distributed in the USA and Canada by
Sterling Publishing Co., Inc.
387 Park Avenue South
New York, NY 10016-8810

For information about custom editions, special sales, premium and corporate purchases, please
contact Sterling Special Sales Department at 800-805-5489 or specialsales@sterlingpub.com.

CONTENTS

INTRODUCTION

With approximately thirteen million adherents, Judaism today is one of the smallest of the world's religions. However, it has had an influence and a geographical distribution inversely proportional to its size. Its origins lie in the state religion of the ancient kingdom of Judah, which came to an end in 586BCE (see pp.12–13). The surviving Judeans faced the challenge of adapting their national religion for an exiled community scattered from Egypt to Mesopotamia. Their success is indicated both by the development of Judaism itself and by the profound formative influence of the Jewish tradition on two other great faiths, Christianity and Islam.

The Diaspora ("dispersion") after 586BCE took Judaism to most corners of the world; and the religion has since developed under the influence of its host cultures. The influence has been mutual, because Jews have served as great transmitters of knowledge.

Judaism has three essential elements: God, Torah, and Israel. Arguably the oldest monotheistic faith, it believes in one universal and eternal God, the creator and sovereign of all that exists. God has entered into a special relationship, or covenant, with one people, the Jews, or Israel, and given them the task of being a "light to the nations" (Isaiah 49.6). There is no expectation in

Judaism that all people will become Jewish, but the hope exists that the whole world will come to acknowledge the sovereignty of the one God. In return for God's care for Israel, Jews have a responsibility to adhere to the divine teachings, or Torah (see pp.38–47). This is the plane on which God and Israel meet. It contains the ethical and ritual commandments (*mitzvot*) through the performance of which one may partake of God's holiness.

The term "Israel" denotes an historic political entity, a people, a nation, a belief system, a social group, and a culture. Its lack of a single clear definition is one reason why there continues to be so much debate among Jews on the question of who *is* a Jew (see p.9). Born as the religion of a specific nation-state, Judaism has had to cope through centuries of exile with the issue of multiple identities. While the religion has served as the basis of Jewish identity, a great role has also been played by a shared historical consciousness and a global ethnic solidarity. In pointing the way toward the redemptive future, Judaism is in constant dialogue with its history.

The Bible records the foundational events in Jewish historical memory: God's promise of land and descendents to Abraham, the Exodus from Egypt, and the entering into a national covenant with God at Mount Sinai. Even though God was eventually to punish the Israelites with

Scenes from the story of the Exodus from Egypt showing the enslaved Israelites and (bottom right) Moses and Aaron confronting the pharaoh. Golden Haggadah, *ca. 1320–1330CE.*

the loss of their national sanctuary and homeland, they always retained the hope that true repentance would lead to the restoration of their relationship with the divine. As God had cared for them in the past, so too would he care for them in the present and the future, as long as they fulfilled his commandments.

All too often the story of the Jews has been presented as a litany of disasters. Since the Hellenistic period (330–63BCE), Jewish distinctiveness has often been subject to derision and incomprehension. Muslim regimes sometimes persecuted Jews, but Christian Europe made anti-Judaism a matter of common policy. For a faith still reeling from the effects of the Nazi persecution (1933–1945), this attention to Jewish suffering throughout the ages is understandable, but it is a precarious foundation upon which to base an identity. Hence there has been a tendency among Jews in recent years to accentuate the positive aspects of Jewish existence. Greater attention is being paid to the significant literary creations of Judaism: the Bible, the Talmud, poetry, philosophy, theology, and ethics. At the same time, this is a period of great creativity, while many formerly non-practicing Jews are rediscovering the essential joy inherent in living a Jewish life.

A major factor in the rediscovery of a "positive Judaism" has been the creation of the state of Israel. Political questions and the issue of defining a Jew and Judaism are undeniably a source of tensions between Israel and the Diaspora communities. Nonetheless, the state of Israel is one of the poles around which modern Jewish life revolves. Often more concerned with external existential matters, Judaism is now confident enough to turn to internal issues of religious and ethnic importance. This attention to inner Jewish concerns is a sign of health and hope for a fruitful future.

CHAPTER ONE

ORIGINS AND HISTORICAL DEVELOPMENT

The ancestors of the Jews first appear on the historical stage in ca. 1200BCE. Since losing their eponymous homeland in 586BCE, the Jews have lived in a creative tension between their homeland and their Diaspora, scattered across the globe and more often than not subject to the whims of their overlords. Nonetheless, they have managed to retain their identity in the face of tremendous adversity. In addition, their status as a minority under both Christianity and Islam thrust them into the role of intermediaries between the cultures. Although the lot of the Jews seemed to improve during the nineteenth century, the twentieth century proved bittersweet, both plunging them into the depths of the Holocaust and inspiring them with the rebirth of their political independence in their ancient homeland.

LEFT: A detail from the synagogue floor in Jericho (7th century CE), depicting ancient Jewish symbols, including the menorah *(7-branched candelabrum),* the shofar *(ram's horn), and the* lulav *(palm-frond). The Star of David did not enter Jewish symbolism until the late medieval period (see p.75).*

The origins of ancient Israel's religion, the precursor of later Judaism, are shrouded in mystery. While some scholars continue to adhere closely to the biblical story, in which the ancestors of Israel introduced a pure monotheism at the beginning of the nation's history, the dominant tendency nowadays is to presuppose a lengthy development in Israel's religion from an originally polytheistic or henotheistic to a monotheistic system by the time of the Babylonian Exile.

The earliest known extra-biblical reference to the Israelites is on the so-called "Israel Stele" of Pharaoh Merneptah of Egypt (ruled ca. 1213–1203BCE). An inscription of the ninth century BCE mentions David as the founder of a dynasty; but the legendary glories of his empire have not been attested archeologically. After the death of Solomon, the kingdom split into two rival states, Israel in the north and Judah in the south. Until its destruction by the Assyrians in 722BCE, Israel was the larger, richer, and more significant state. However, since the Bible was written by scribes of Judean descent, it presents a consistently negative image of the northern kingdom. Its assessment of Judah is more varied, although its judgments are based on theological rather than political criteria. In 586BCE, Nebuchadnezzar of Babylon conquered Judah, destroyed its central Temple of Jerusalem (see pp.68–9), and deported members of the upper classes. Nonetheless, the exiles retained their national religion, setting a precedent for Judaism as an exilic faith during centuries of dispersal.

In order to retain their identity, the exiled Judeans—"Judean" is the original meaning of the term "Jew"—were forced to adapt their religion. The Judean national God, YHWH, was reinterpreted as the universal God of all human history. Hence the disasters that had befallen the Judeans did not represent the triumph of Babylon and its deities, but the punishment of the Judeans by the one God. This theology in turn led to a re-examination of the relationship between the divine and the human and of the ritual and ethical demands this entailed. Intertwined with these issues was the need to preserve the exiles' ancient traditions. Thus began the Jewish scholarly tradition that in the first instance gave birth to many of the writings of the Bible (see pp.38–45).

Under Persian rule, those who wished were allowed to return home and restore their religious practices. Judaism again had a central sanctuary and a degree of self-government, and so began the pattern whereby a Jewish presence in the land of Israel coexisted with Jewish communities in the outside world, collectively known as the Diaspora ("dispersal").

After Judea came under Greek rule, the successors of Alexander the Great continued his policy of Hellenization, imposing Greek culture on their domains. In the religious sphere, this included identifying the deities of conquered peoples with those of the Greek pantheon. Jewish society was split between Hellenists, who advocated a rapid accommodation of the essentially very open and tolerant Hellenistic system, and pietists, who saw it as inimical to the exclusive monotheism of Judaism. The Greek ruler Antiochus IV Epiphanes (175–164BCE) sided with the Jewish Hellenists and acted against the Jewish religion. Led by the priest Mattathias and his son Judah Maccabee (Judas Maccabeus), the pietists rebelled, won back a measure of Judean autonomy, and rededicated the defiled Temple in 164BCE (see also p.83). Ironically, the Hasmonean dynasty founded by the rebels itself became a strong advocate of Hellenic culture until, wracked by corruption, Judea fell to the Romans in 63BCE.

Judaism, as it is known and practiced today, has its roots in the upheavals of early Roman Palestine. Initially, the Romans governed through a Jewish client dynasty founded by Herod the Great (37–4BCE), a ruthless but effective ruler held in suspicion by many Jews as a descendant of forced converts to Judaism. His reign was marked by an ambitious building program that included rebuilding the Second Temple on a grand scale.

Following Herod's death, Judea was governed for several decades by oppressive Roman prefects The Jews finally rose up against the occupying power in 66CE, but after some initial successes, the revolt (the First Jewish War) succumbed to the overwhelming might of imperial Rome. Jerusalem was captured and the Temple razed (70CE). One more attempt to break Roman control over Palestine (the Bar Kokhba revolt, or Second Jewish War, 132–135CE) ended with the temporary banishment of Jews from Jerusalem. Jewish national aspirations were effectively shattered until the twentieth century.

While Jerusalem was under siege during the First Jewish War, a rabbi, Yohanan ben Zakkai, received permission from the Romans to found an academy of Jewish learning. He saw that Judaism's future lay not in taking arms against Rome, but in the scholastic tradition represented by the Pharisees, who were one of a number of Jewish sects that existed during the late Second Temple period (164BCE–70CE), which also included the Sadducees, Essenes, Zealots, and the Jesus movement.

Pharisaic Judaism was characterized by a belief not only in the written Torah (the Bible) but also in the "oral Torah," laws handed down verbally since God first vouchsafed them to Moses and adapted to changing circumstances (see pp.42–3). The Pharisees democratized Jewish learning, in that their academies were open to all men, and their ideal of the rabbi was one trained in a trade. Their belief in an afterlife allowed them to accept their often difficult lot in this world.

Within a few years, the center of Jewish life and learning in the land of Israel had shifted to Galilee, in whose academies generations of scholars debated the minutiae of Jewish custom and law. This process was mirrored outside Palestine in the great Jewish academies of Babylon, which produced an outstanding achievement ca. 500CE in the form of the Babylonian Talmud, the most influential work in Judaism since the Bible (see p.42). Judaism had entered a long period of scholarly introspection, during which its adherents for the most part lived a precarious existence as a minority among often hostile dominant cultures.

At the height of the Roman empire it is estimated that one tenth of the population of Rome was Jewish. In addition, a large number of gentiles (non-Jews) were attracted to Judaism, but did not convert because of their difficulty with such requirements as male circumcision. A Jewish offshoot, Christianity, did not enforce such specifically Jewish laws, and proved a more attractive alternative for many gentiles drawn to ethical monotheism. Christianity became the Roman state religion in 392CE, and thereafter Christian rulers enacted discriminatory laws designed to make explicit God's supposed rejection of the Jews.

The history of the Jews in Christendom is one of nearly constant persecution. Massacres, expulsions, and forced conversions were common, and Jews were blamed for natural disasters such as the Black Death (1348–9). Excluded from most professions, European Jews were more often than not obliged to become merchants and moneylenders. Long restricted in their choice of domicile, from the sixteenth century, Jews began to be sequestered in special town quarters, called "ghettos" after the area of Venice where the first was situated.

The position of the Jews under Islam could also be precarious, but in times of tolerance they flourished in a manner unthinkable under Christian rule, becoming doctors, merchants, court officials, scientists, and poets. The high point in this respect was the "Golden Age" of the Jews of Muslim Spain (tenth–twelfth centuries CE).

The general division between Sephardi ("Spanish") and Ashkenazi ("German") Jewry goes back to the Middle Ages, although in most cases, the connection with the "homeland" has long been forgotten. After

The minstrel Suesskind of Trimberg wearing a "Jew's hat" that sets him apart from the majority culture as he addresses Christian authorities. (Manesse Codex, 14th century.)

their expulsion from Spain, the Sephardim went to the Netherlands, North Africa, Italy, and the Ottoman empire; some even found their way to the Americas.

The Ashkenazim initially lived along the Rhine, but these vibrant communities were devastated by the First

Crusade in 1096. They reconstituted themselves, but the center of Jewish life in northern Europe shifted to the east. By the twentieth century, the greatest concentration of Ashkenazim was in Poland and Russia, despite a harsh life there. Most of these communities ended with mass emigration (mainly to the United States) and the Holocaust. A third major group, often included with the Sephardim, consists of Jews whose ancestors stayed in the Middle East, the Edot ha-Mizrah ("Communities of the East") or Mizrahim ("Easterners"). For over a millennium, the Jewish community of Babylon was Judaism's leading light. Another important group lived in Yemen. Most Jews of these communities fled or emigrated to Israel after 1948.

Jews played an important role as mediators between the cultures. Since there were Jewish communities scattered across Europe, Asia, and North Africa, Jews were an integral part of international trade and, as a consequence of their linguistic skills, a major conduit of learning. Indeed, it has been argued that Arab learning disseminated by Jews expelled from Spain in 1492 was a major factor in stimulating the European renaissance.

The pressures of life in western and central Europe led to the movement of large numbers of Jews into eastern Europe, where things proved little better. As their situation grew more desperate, an increasing number of Jews turned to mysticism and messianic speculation as a source of hope in a hostile world. A number of false messiahs arose, the most famous being Shabbetai Zvi, or Tzvi (1626–76), of Smyrna in Turkey (see p.33).

From the eighteenth century, the situation of Jews as the outcasts of Christian European society seemed to take a turn for the better, during the Enlightenment and the subsequent emancipation of the Jews in many countries. For the first time, they were accorded equal civil rights in some western European states and in the New World. However, full acceptance came only with baptism, and many Jews purchased their entry into general society at the price of their Judaism. Those not willing to renounce Judaism were the driving force behind the Jewish reform movement of the early nineteenth century. While some applauded the radical innovations of the reformers, others considered them to be renegades from true Judaism. The result was the division of Judaism into the three major movements of today: Reform, Conservative, and Orthodox (see pp.98–103).

In the late nineteenth century, the development of racial supremacist theories derived from Darwinian evolutionary thought gave rise to a new form of anti-Judaism, namely anti-Semitism, a term first coined by a

German political agitator in 1879 to redefine Jew-hatred on racial rather than religious grounds. Anti-Semitism is now used to designate any occurrence of anti-Judaism, whether it be motivated by race, religion, or politics. The lamentable success of anti-Semitism is indicated by its adoption by the virulently anti-Jewish racist political movements of the late nineteenth and early twentieth centuries, including, most notoriously, Hitler's National Socialists (Nazis). This baleful phenomenon reached its peak in the murder of two-thirds of European Jewry— one-third of the entire Jewish people—during the Holocaust (1941–45), the name given to the systematic mass slaughter that marked the climax of the anti-Semitic policies of Nazi Germany (1933–45).

Jewish aspirations did not end with this disaster. Another Jewish movement, Zionism, had been founded by Theodor Herzl (see p.55) at the end of the nineteenth century. Taking its name from Zion, the ancient poetic name of Jerusalem, it sought a solution to the age-old "Jewish question" in the return of the Jews to their homeland in Palestine and their revitalization as a nation. In 1948, following the United Nations Partition Plan of the previous year, a Jewish national entity was established in the land of Israel, bringing to an end nearly 1,900 years of Jewish disenfranchisement.

Principles of Life in the Diaspora

❝ Thus says YHWH of Hosts, the God of Israel, to all of the exilic community that I have exiled from Jerusalem to Babylon: Build houses and dwell [in them], plant gardens and eat their fruit. Take wives [for yourselves] and beget sons and daughters; take wives for your sons, and give your daughters to men, so they may bear sons and daughters. Increase in number there, and do not decrease. Seek the well-being of the city to which I have exiled you, and pray to YHWH on its behalf. For through its well-being will you know peace. **❞**

Jeremiah 29.4–7, translated by Carl S. Ehrlich.

Commentary

Born of an outcast priestly family, the prophet Jeremiah was an opponent of the entrenched religious and political leadership. The last rulers of Judah played a dangerous game of shifting alliances between Egypt and Babylonia. In spite of Jeremiah's warnings, the kings of Judah repeatedly took up arms against the Babylonians and were punished by having the sitting ruler deposed and exiled to Babylon along with other members of the upper classes in 597BCE, and by losing their national independence and having their central sanctuary in

Jerusalem destroyed in 586BCE. Once again, the leading members of society were deported to Babylon. Jeremiah himself avoided exile to Babylon, only to end his days as a refugee from Babylonian reprisals in Egypt.

Contrary to expectations, many of the exiled and refugee Judeans managed to avoid assimilation in Babylon. This was largely due to the efforts of religious leaders like Jeremiah and his younger contemporary Ezekiel, who argued that it was possible to retain both religious and national identity even in exile. Thus was born the bifurcation that has marked Judaism since that time, the division of the Jewish people into a community in the national homeland and one living in the Diaspora ("dispersion").

Jeremiah's "Letter to the Exiles" represents an important stage in the development of a Diaspora identity. According to this letter, Jeremiah established a successful blueprint for Jewish existence. While retaining a connection to the ancient homeland, Jews were to become loyal citizens of the lands in which they lived. Their welfare was dependent on that of their new homeland. The rabbinic dictum that "the law of the land is the law" is an extension of this principle. Only by obeying the laws of the land, could Jewish life and community prosper, even if it occasionally meant infractions against some of the hedges around the Torah.

CHAPTER TWO

ASPECTS OF THE DIVINE

Judaism conceives of its God as the one and only universal deity. The Jewish people and their God are bound through a covenant—a formal relationship which regulates Jewish patterns of behavior and ethics. God is viewed as the ultimate reality behind creation, an invisible, indivisible, and transcendent deity who is the source of morality and ethics. In spite of his omniscience and omnipotence, he has limited his direct involvement in human affairs, in order to allow humanity the exercise of free will. Nonetheless, a distinctly Jewish contribution to general theology is the messianic idea, which holds that God will eventually intervene directly in human affairs to redeem the world. His absence during the horrors of the Holocaust has led, however, to a crisis in modern Jewish thought.

LEFT: Since the 18th century, richly decorated tablets, inscribed with Psalm 16:8 and other verses in which the name of God is prominent, were often placed in front of worshippers in the synagogue. These tablets are known as Shiviti—the one shown here is an American paper-cut, dated 1861.

The ancient Israelites conceived of their relationship with God as a covenant. The Bible speaks of different types of covenant (Hebrew *brit*) with God. One is the personal relationship between an individual and God, marked in males by the rite of circumcision (*brit milah*). Another is the covenant between the people and God, which is symbolized by the pact entered into at Mount Sinai. The Sinaitic covenant between God and Israel is modelled on ancient Near Eastern treaties in which an overlord entered into a formal relationship with a vassal. In return for God's deliverance of the Israelites from bondage, they acknowledged the suzerainty of God by observing the divine commandments. The fulfillment of the commandments is hence viewed as Judaism's obligation to God, who is in turn obliged to care for the Jews. The breach of this mutual relationship by either party is considered an unjustifiable transgression.

The exclusive relationship between Israel and God is expressed in the Shema prayer, which has become the central Jewish confession of faith. It is so called from the first word of Deuteronomy 6.4: "Hear (Shema), O Israel, YHWH is our God, YHWH alone" (or, "YHWH is our God, YHWH is one"). In the expanded version of the prayer, this single verse is augmented by other verses from Deuteronomy and Numbers. (See also pp.34–5.)

As the creator, God is the ultimate reality behind all earthly existence, a god of history who endows history with a moral sense. The essence of God is goodness, but Judaism is not dualistic: that is, God is the creator of both good and evil. In addressing the issue of why evil and suffering exist in the world, theologians have employed the notion of *tzimtzum* ("self-limitation") to explain the temporary triumph of the human inclination to evil. But the enormity of the Holocaust has provoked a crisis in Jewish theology, with some thinkers questioning both the nature and even the existence of God.

Judaism conceives of God as transcendent, above nature and the world. However, the deity is present in the world in the sense that he communicates with people through various media. The kabbalistic ("mystical") tradition of *tzimtzum* holds that God, while remaining omniscient and omnipotent, has voluntarily relinquished some control over the world, bestowing free will on humanity in order to give it the chance to prove its own level of maturity.

Judaism emphasizes that humanity is forced to resort to limiting language and metaphors to characterize a God who is inherently beyond the capacity of words to describe. The best one can do is to list, discuss, and learn from God's attributes, the two most important of which are justice and mercy. These have been likened in some contemporary Jewish circles to the male and female aspects of God. Just as God must be prepared to reward and punish his children like a father, so too must the deity exhibit compassion for her children like a mother.

The God of Israel also has a name, which was in common usage during the biblical period. This is the "Tetragrammaton," the ineffable four-letter name of God, represented in Hebrew by the consonants YHWH (see illustration, opposite). In postbiblical Judaism, YHWH was considered too holy to be uttered, and substitutes were found to avoid having to speak it. The most common is *Adonai* ("my Lord"). In some Jewish circles, *Adonai* itself has become too holy to be pronounced, except in prayer, and so other circumlocutions have come to be used, such as *ha-Shem* ("the Name"). Alternative ways of referring to God include recitations of divine attributes (such as "the Holy One" and "the Merciful One"). God's presence in the world is designated the *Shekhinah*, a feminine noun that has been the source of much Jewish mystical speculation regarding God's male and female aspects. The *Shekhinah* has also become an important concept in feminist theology (see pp.104–5).

Unlike the deities of the pagan world, which were depicted in various animal and anthropomorphic forms,

The Tetragrammaton, the four-letter name of God, is at the center of this Hebrew Bible illumination, copied in Spain in 1384CE.

the God of Judaism is formless, invisible, and beyond the capacity of human beings to comprehend. Since its earliest days, Judaism has been concerned to emphasize this by avoiding artistic portrayals that might be confused with attempts to depict the deity. The prohibition is codified in the Second Commandment (Exodus 20.4–6, Deuteronomy 5.8–10).

The interpretation of this commandment has caused tensions between those Jews who would ban representational art in general (iconoclasts) and those who would permit it in almost any setting. During the late Roman and Byzantine periods, rabbis who would not have allowed iconography in their divine ritual worshipped in synagogues with beautiful mosaic floors and, at least at Dura-Europos in Syria, walls adorned with biblical scenes. Some mosaics even depicted such non-Jewish scenes as the Greek sun god Helios. But the Jewish context was considered to deprive such images of any original religious significance and they could thus serve as representations of the universal cycle of life. Over the centuries, the pendulum has swung between the extremes. However, as the wealth of Jewish illustration throughout history has shown, Judaism has always had some form of artistic tradition.

In opposition to more rational ways of approaching the divine, there have long existed strong mystical currents in Judaism. The most influential of such movements has been Kabbalah, in which the study of an intricate set of symbols is meant to lead the initiate closer to the ultimate divine reality (see p.47).

One intersection between the divine and the human spheres is sought in the concept of a messiah. The messianic idea developed in Judaism as a response to national catastrophe, offering hope to a people whose circumstances were often precarious. The word "messiah" itself is a transcription of the Hebrew *mashiah*, "one who is anointed" with oil for a specific purpose by God. In the Bible, a variety of individuals are termed "messiahs" by virtue of being anointed, including kings, priests, prophets, and even non-Israelites. But the Bible does not link these figures with the later concept of *the* Messiah who would initiate the redemptive end of time, although passages have often been employed to support one or another messianic vision.

By the late Second Temple period, diverse hopes for the future centering around a descendent of the house of David had combined in various ways with aspects of apocalyptic thought. The result was the idea of an imminent messiah who would either personally save the Jews from oppression and usher in the rule of God, or would rule in glory after God had saved the Jews. As Herodian and Roman rule grew more oppressive, a number of messianic claimants arose, such as Simeon bar Kokhba, who led the Jews in a failed anti-Roman revolt (the Second Jewish War, 132–135CE). Most rabbis rejected the claims made on his behalf; an exception was the great Akiva (see p.53). It is unclear whether Jesus of Nazareth considered himself to be the messiah, but enough of his followers did so to call him *christos* ("Christ"), the Greek for *mashiah*.

Although the Dead Sea Scrolls already mention the idea of dual (priestly and royal) messiahs, it may have been in the aftermath of the Bar Kokhba revolt that the concept developed of two messiahs, one descended from the house of the patriarch Joseph and one from the house of David. The messiah descended from David, whose rule would signal the establishment of God's kingdom on earth, would be preceded by one descended from the patriarch Joseph, who would lead the forces of good against the forces of evil in a doomed struggle. His failure and death would be the prelude to God's intervention in history, when he would establish his rule under the second, Davidic, messiah.

One tradition claims that the messiah was created at the beginning of time and is waiting with God until the moment of redemption. According to another theory, a potential human messiah walks the earth in every generation. There is even a tradition that a leprous, begging messiah sits at the gates of Rome waiting for his moment in history. The great Jewish rationalist philosopher Maimonides (see pp.56–7) rejected the idea of a messiah who would act outside the bounds of normal human history, and fought against the apocalypticists who would have the messiah usher in the end of time. Nevertheless, he formulated a belief in the coming of the messiah as one of his thirteen articles of Jewish faith.

Most messianic movements were confined to a particular time and place, but one convulsed the whole of the Jewish world. In 1665, Shabbetai Zvi, or Tzvi (1626–76), a wandering mystic who was born in Smyrna in Turkey, appeared in the land of Israel, where he was proclaimed the messiah by the visionary Nathan of Gaza.

Shabbetai was hailed throughout the Jewish world, so recently demoralized by the dreadful Cossack pogroms led by Bogdan Chmielnicki in 1648–9 in the Ukraine. Jews everywhere prepared for the coming kingdom of God, but within the same year, Shabbetai had been jailed by the sultan and had converted to Islam rather than be executed. Yet he still retained followers who viewed his conversion as the necessary degradation of the messiah before his ultimate glorious triumph. However, for most Jews, Shabbetai illustrates the wisdom of the first-century Rabbi Yohanan ben Zakkai, who said that if you are about to plant a sapling when someone tells you the messiah has come, of course go out to greet the messiah—but plant the sapling first.

A Declaration of Faith

❝ Listen Israel, YHWH is our God, only YHWH. You shall love YHWH, your God, whole heartedly, with your whole life, and with your whole being. These words that I command you today shall be upon your heart. You shall teach them to your children and speak of them when you reside in your home and when you are on a journey, when you lie down and when you get up. You shall tie them as a symbol on your arm, and they will serve as signs between your eyes. You shall inscribe them upon the doorposts of your house and on your gates. **❞**

Deuteronomy 6.4–9, translated by Carl S. Ehrlich.

Commentary

The Shema prayer, so called on the basis of the first word, which means "listen" or "hear," is recited during morning and evening prayers and, emulating Rabbi Akiva (see p.53), also on one's deathbed. Although the Shema in its original seventh-century BCE context may have meant that among all the gods, the Judeans should only worship YHWH (henotheism), Judaism has come to understand the Shema as its central declaration of faith in one indivisible God (monotheism).

In a liturgical context, the Shema and its blessings make up one of the major portions of the synagogue service. The Shema in its long form consists of the Shema itself (Deut. 6.4), the following verses (Deut. 6.5–9), known as the *Ve-ahavta* ("You shall love"), and two additional biblical passages (Deut. 11.13–21 and Num. 14.37–41), which deal respectively with obedience to the commandments and with the commandment to put fringes on the corners of one's garments.

The love for God that one is supposed to internalize is an expression of loyalty. The importance of handing down the tradition from one generation to another is encapsulated for Judaism by the enjoinder to teach one's children. The directive to recite these words upon lying down and rising up determined the recitation of the Shema at both the evening and the morning services, as well as the custom to recite it upon waking up and just before going to sleep. Judaism also has understood the concluding injunctions in a literal manner. Hence, the text opposite is to be found written on parchment and placed in little boxes (*tefillin*, "phylacteries") strapped on one's arm and dangling between one's eyes at the morningservice. It is also to be found in small containers (*mezuzot*, sing. *mezuzah*) affixed to doorposts in Jewish buildings and homes (see p.74).

CHAPTER THREE

SACRED TEXTS

Religious literature plays a central role in Jewish life and thought. The primary book of Judaism, and the ultimate source for its rituals and ethics, is the Torah, which is accorded special reverence in the synagogue setting. The Torah is also the first of the three parts of the Hebrew Bible. Characteristic of Judaism is its continuing engagement with its ancient traditions. Thus, additional literary works which comment on and explicate Jewish tradition, as first codified in the Torah, have also assumed great importance. Foremost among these has been the Talmud, which itself has given rise to a rich interpretative tradition. Other important theological works include the Siddur ("prayerbook"), the Haggadah (a manual for the celebration of the Passover meal), and the *Zohar* (the foundational text of Jewish mysticism).

LEFT: The Shrine of the Book at the Israel Museum in Jerusalem houses the Dead Sea Scrolls, among which are to be found the oldest manuscripts of the books of the Hebrew Bible. The centerpiece of the shrine is a complete scroll of the Book of Isaiah (2nd century BCE–1st century CE).

The primary religious text of Judaism is the Torah, a word often translated as "law" but originally meaning "teaching" or "instruction." In its narrow sense, the Torah is the first five books of the Bible, also known as the Five Books of Moses and the Pentateuch. From the Torah, the rabbis of the Talmudic age (ca. second–seventh centuries CE) distilled the six hundred and thirteen commandments that form the building blocks of Jewish life and custom.

"Torah" is also often taken to refer to the whole Bible, which consists of three parts. Following the Pentateuch, the second section is referred to as the Prophets (Nevi'im) and contains both narrative and prophetic books. Thirdly, there are the eleven books known as the Writings (Ketuvim), or Hagiographa, a miscellany of poetry, wisdom, prophecy, and history. Another designation for the Bible is Tanakh, an acronym derived from the initial letters of Torah, Nevi'im, and Ketuvim.

The tripartite division of the Hebrew Bible reflects not only the order in which it was canonized, but also the relative importance of the texts in Jewish tradition. The Pentateuch, the Torah proper, has pride of place both as the ultimate source of Jewish beliefs and practices and as an object of veneration. Each community's Torah scrolls are housed in the synagogue in a special niche or ark in one wall, toward which worshippers pray, traditionally in the direction of Jerusalem. A different portion, or *parashah*, of the Torah scroll is recited in the synagogue each week, so that the whole Torah is read out in either an annual or a triennial cycle. After the *parashah*, a shorter passage from the Prophets is read as a complement. The synagogue reading from the Scriptures has given rise to another Hebrew term for the Bible, Miqra' ("That which is read [aloud]"), a direct cognate of the Arabic Qur'an.

The Sefer Torah (Torah Scroll) is the most sacred object in Judaism. Each letter of the scroll must be painstakingly handwritten by a *sofer* (scribe), who will have trained for around seven years. The Torah is written on parchment made from the skin of a *kosher* animal (see p.63) and takes about a year to complete. After being thoroughly checked by the *sofer* and other experts, an Ashkenazi scroll is covered ("dressed") in an embroidered protective "mantle," which is often richly decorated, especially with crowns. Silver finials, or *rimmonim* (Hebrew, "pomegranates") may also be placed over the scroll handles. In the Sephardic community, Torah scrolls are encased in decorated wooden or metal cylinders lined with velvet.

The Torah Scroll remains dressed at all times when not in use for readings. In reciting from the scroll, the

Like the Torah Scroll, the Book of Esther (shown here; Italian, 18th century) is often handwritten as a scroll. However, unlike the Torah, it is generally lavishly illustrated.

reader may follow the text with a pointer, or *yad* (Hebrew, "hand"), to avoid touching the scriptures. The *yad* is often made of silver, but can also be made of ivory or wood. If even a single letter is erased over time, the scroll becomes unsuitable for use until a *sofer* has restored the letter. A scroll that has become too worn for restoration is taken to a Jewish cemetery for burial.

The destruction of the First Temple in Jerusalem in 586BCE and of the Second Temple in 70CE, with their accompanying losses of national identity, forced the Jews in each instance to compile their traditions in written form in order to ensure their survival. This led in the first case to the redaction of large portions of the Torah and Prophets, and in the second to the compilation of the oral traditions which were eventually to find their way into the Mishnah and hence also into the Talmud. Yohanan ben Zakkai (see p.15) recognized that the key to the survival of Judaism lay in the transmission of Jewish learning and the transfer of the symbols of the Temple religion to other aspects of Jewish life. In his academy at Yavneh, and in others that followed it, the rabbis developed a system of law and custom through an intense discussion of Jewish tradition and its adaptation to changing circumstances. These rabbinic decisions, or "oral law," covering all aspects of religious and secular life, were codified ca. 200CE by Rabbi Judah the Prince in the Mishnah ("That Which Is Taught"), which is divided into six "orders" and subdivided into sixty-three "tractates."

The Mishnah itself became the basis for further discussion in the various Jewish communities. The wide-ranging rabbinic debates on the Mishnah, including both majority and minority opinions, were themselves compiled in the Talmud of Jerusalem (ca. 400CE) and the

Talmud of Babylon (ca. 500CE). The Babylonian Talmud became the standard collection of Jewish traditions. The two Talmuds use the same Mishnah text, but differ in their record of the debates, or Gemara. The Talmud ("Study") has attained the status of a holy text, of equal stature in the rabbinic view, to the Bible. A whole literature of additions (Tosafot), commentaries, and super-commentaries has continued down to the modern era.

Following the injunction in the tractate *Pirke Avot* ("Sayings of the Fathers") to "build a hedge [or fence] around the Torah," the rabbis attempted to safeguard it with additional regulations and customs. In theory, it was considered less serious to violate one of the "hedges" than one of the primary six hundred and thirteen commandments of the Torah proper. In practice, the immediacy of the newer regulation often ensured that it was honored as greatly as—indeed, if not more than—the original proscription.

Rabbinic tradition places the so-called "oral Torah," the talmudic legacy, on the same level as the written Torah. Both are said to have been divinely given to Moses at Mount Sinai. The written Torah was revealed to all of Israel. The oral Torah was handed down by a circle of initiates until its compilation in writing many centuries later by the rabbis. Thus "Torah" can refer to both the biblical and the talmudic traditions and, in its widest sense, to the totality of Jewish law and custom. Because it was in book form, Jews could carry this "portable homeland" wherever they went.

In formulating the belief that the oral Torah was revealed at Mount Sinai at the same time as the written Torah, the rabbis of the talmudic age established the important and influential principle that the development of Jewish law and tradition was as much a part of the revealed message as the Torah itself. The centrality of this tenet is illustrated most graphically in the story in which Moses is said to attend the academy of the great scholar Rabbi Akiva (see p.53). Moses is unable to understand any part of the discussion until a student bases his argument on the Torah proper, the books written by Moses himself. It is then that Moses comprehends that the tradition he passed on to Israel is not monolithic and static, but subject to change and modification over time.

Traditional Jewish interpretation is usually in accordance with the scholarly method known as *midrash* ("inquiry" or "investigation"), the examination of a biblical text in order to derive either legal insights (*midrash halakhah*) or homiletic ones (*midrash aggadah*). The *midrash aggadah* has been the more beloved and generally accessible. The text of the Talmud contains both of these approaches to interpretation, and the midrashic method is still employed today in reworking the tradition for a new age.

In a traditional Jewish context, the Bible is not read on its own. For example, rabbinic Bibles (*Miqra'ot Gedolot*) juxtapose commentaries from different ages and countries, beginning with that of Rashi (Rabbi Solomon ben Isaac, 1040–1105CE; see pp.53–4) from northern France, with the text of the Bible in Hebrew and Aramaic. The reader is thus invited to become a participant in the ancient and continuing discussion of the meaning of the biblical text. Such investigation aims not to arrive at a definitive interpretation, but rather to expand one's knowledge of the interpretative possibilities, in recognition that truth is always multilayered.

Over the centuries, the exposition of the legal aspects of Jewish tradition has spawned an extensive commentary literature, adding super-commentaries to commentaries on the traditional texts. There have also been attempts to codify Jewish legal traditions. Of these law codes, the most famous and influential were the *Mishneh Torah* ("Repetition of the Torah") of Maimonides (see pp.56–7) and the *Shulhan Arukh* ("Set Table") of Joseph Caro (1488–1575). These codes organize Jewish practice by subject-matter and hence can be used as reference tools. In effect, they cover all aspects of life from a Jewish perspective.

Alongside these comprehensive attempts to present the totality of Jewish practice, collections were made of answers (*responsa*) given by rabbis to questions that arose from people's daily lives as Jews. This literature continues to be augmented today, most poignantly with the publication of *responsa* written during the Holocaust and reflecting the desire of Jews to continue to follow a Jewish way of life, even under extreme duress.

A passage in the Talmud concludes that the study of the Torah is equal in merit to all other ethical activities, because it is the gateway that leads to them all. This preoccupation with the study and practice of the Torah in all its aspects has ensured the continued vitality and survival of Judaism over the course of the millennia.

Two additional books stand out from all others owing to their importance in the context of Jewish life and ritual. The first is the Siddur, or prayerbook. There are many versions of the Siddur for daily, Sabbath, or holiday prayers. There are also differences between Ashkenazi and Sephardi versions, as well as between those of the Orthodox, Conservative, and

Reform movements. However, all these versions share a certain basic, identifiable, structure and liturgy.

After the preliminary prayers, which set the spiritual tone for what follows, comes the first important part of the service. This section revolves around the Shema prayer (Deuteronomy 6.4), the central Jewish confession of faith in the one God (see pp.34–5), beginning with a call to worship. God is then praised as the creator. God's love for Israel and Israel's acceptance of the Torah provide the background for the hope in an eventual redemption. The next part of the service is known as the Amidah ("Standing"), since it is customary to stand while reciting this prayer. It consists in its weekday version of nineteen benedictions, thanking God for providing for both the individual and the community. The service ends with the Aleinu, a prayer which looks forward to a time when the world will be united in belief in one God, and the mourners' recitation of the Kaddish, a prayer extolling God, which also acts as a divider between the other parts of the service (see pp.94–5).

The second book is the Haggadah, the "Recounting" of the story of the Exodus of the Israelites under Moses from Egypt. The book serves as the basis of the family's ceremonial Passover meal (Seder), during which God's great act of liberation is recited and relived from generation to generation.

The Haggadah intersperses the biblical narrative with rabbinic interpretation and *midrash*. It is designed to be didactic and to hold the interest of children; it therefore plays a significant role in the formation of their Jewish identity.

A collection of late thirteenth-century Aramaic writings called the *Zohar* ("Illumination") is the foundational text of Kabbalah, Judaism's most influential mystical movement. The *Zohar* was most likely written by the Spanish mystic Moses de León (died 1305), who claimed to have compiled it from the writings of a celebrated rabbi of the second century CE, Simeon bar Yohai.

In its attempt to penetrate the mystery of the deity, Kabbalah drew on the *Zohar* to develop a complex concept of God as consisting of an unknowable central mystery (the *Ein Sof*) and ten aspects (*Sefirot*). To this was attached an intricate symbolism, the study of which led the initiate closer to understanding ultimate truth.

The Enlightenment and the rise of rationalism decreased the influence of the *Zohar*. However, there has been a rise in Jewish mystical speculation in recent years among ultra-orthodox and Hasidic Jews, as well as among those Jews who have been influenced by New Age and millennial thought or who have otherwise engaged in the modern quest for spirituality.

A *Midrash* on Rabbinic Authority

❞ It is taught that on that very day Rabbi Eliezer presented all the arguments in the world, but the rest of them [rabbis] did not accept them. He said to them, "If the *halakhah* ["religious law"] is as I say, may this carob tree prove it." Thereupon the carob tree was uprooted from where it was a distance of one hundred cubits; some say four hundred cubits. But they said to him, "One doesn't bring proof from a carob tree." ... He [Rabbi Eliezer] continued and said to them, "If the *halakhah* is as I say, may heaven prove it!" Thereupon a heavenly voice resounded and said, "What's your problem with Rabbi Eliezer, with whom the *halakhah* always agrees?" Thereupon Rabbi Joshua stood up on his feet and said, "It is not in heaven" [Deut. 30.12a]. How do we know that it isn't in heaven? Rabbi Jeremiah said, "Because the Torah was already given at Mount Sinai. We don't need to pay attention to a divine voice, since you already wrote in the Torah at Mount Sinai: to decide according to the majority." Once Rabbi Nathan encountered Elijah [the prophet] and asked him, "How did God react at that time?" He answered him, "He [God] smiled and said, 'My children have bested me; my children have bested me!'" ❞

From the *Babylonian Talmud, Tractate Bava Metzia* 59b, translated by Carl S. Ehrlich.

Commentary

This amusing *aggadic midrash* (see p.43) contains both the essence of the rabbinic interpretative process and a profound statement about the relationship between God and humanity. By ascribing divine origin to the "oral law," the rabbis of the talmudic age essentially claimed divine status for their specific interpretative tradition. Even though they stated that their exposition of the laws was given to Moses on Mount Sinai, *midrashim* such as this one make clear that they knew that they were engaged in the radical reformulation of previous traditions. That they were not unanimous in their decisions is indicated by innumerable passages in the Talmud. Nonetheless, their general principle was to let the majority decide how to interpret the traditions, while still recording the minority opinions.

Fully cognizant of their seeming hubris in often going against older traditions that had had divine sanction, the rabbis understood the relationship between God and the Jews as comparable to that of a parent and child. Just as a parent is proud when a child takes what has been taught and learns to act independently, so too is God pleased when his children take his teaching, the Torah, and demonstrate that they are able to understand and apply it on their own.

CHAPTER FOUR

SACRED PERSONS

There have been many influential figures in Judaism who have been revered long after their deaths. But characteristic of the Jewish regard for revered persons is that they remain human—although they may have stood in a special relationship with the divine, they themselves cannot aspire to any measure of divinity. Indeed, Jewish heroes are often depicted as flawed individuals. Not even Moses, the foundational figure of Judaism, was anything more than a man, and it is perhaps to avoid worship of him that the Bible emphasizes that the location of his grave is unknown. Nonetheless, the burial sites of many other significant Jews have become objects of veneration—from the supposed graves of the patriarchs and matriarchs in Hebron to, more recently, the grave of the last Lubavitcher rabbi in New York.

LEFT:
Arguably the greatest figure of the Jewish Middle Ages was the polymath Moses ben Maimon (Maimonides), who was born in Spain, but moved to Egypt. This modern sculpture was erected in his honor in his birthplace of Córdoba, Spain.

In Judaism, although human beings may aspire to holiness through their actions, the veneration of mortals is generally avoided. Figures from the past are objects of emulation, but not adoration: the division between the divine and the human realms remains. There is no apotheosis in Judaism.

Two individuals tower above all others in Jewish tradition: Moses and King David. Although no firm historical statements can be made regarding Moses, he is the central figure in the Torah and of subsequent Judaism. God chose him to free the Israelites from Egyptian bondage and lead them to the Promised Land. Through him the divine covenant with Israel was sealed and the commandments transmitted. Thus Moses is the foundational figure of Judaism and the archetypal Jew.

King David, the second major figure in the Jewish tradition, was revered as a political leader and poet. Although a flawed human being, God nevertheless looked upon him with favor. The legendary golden age of David and his son Solomon is a great source of inspiration for Jews, and is closely bound up with messianic hopes (see pp.30–3).

The prototypical rabbinic Jew was Hillel (first century BCE), the exemplar of Jewish learning infused with a deep humanity and humility. The Talmud relates that when a potential convert asked to be taught the whole of the Torah, Hillel replied: "What is hateful to you, do not do to anyone else. The rest is commentary. Go and study." Rabbi Akiva (ca. 50–135CE), perhaps the greatest scholar of the rabbinic period, was an illiterate shepherd until the age of forty. A follower of the messianic claimant Simeon bar Kokhba (see p.31), Akiva was killed by the Romans, and died uttering the words of the Shema prayer (see pp.34–5), establishing a model of martyrdom for Jews throughout the ages.

The Talmud mentions one woman, Beruriah (second century CE), whose learning, according to tradition, equalled that of any man. Many tales have been told of her wisdom and humanity, and she has inspired generations of Jewish women seeking access to the learning that has traditionally been a male preserve.

The two outstanding sages of the Middle Ages are "Rashi" and "Rambam," acronyms respectively of Rabbi Shlomo Yitzhaki (Solomon ben Isaac, 1040–1105) and Rabbi Moses ben Maimon (or Maimonides, 1135–1204). Rashi spent most of his life in his native Troyes in France, but he studied in Germany and represents the last flowering of Rhineland Jewry before its decimation in the First Crusade. His great achievement lay in making Jewish learning accessible to all through his

Like a Shiviti (see pp.24–5), a Mizrah *("East") indicates the
direction of prayer toward Jerusalem. This one, ca. 1900, shows
Moses carrying the Ten Commandments.*

commentaries on the Bible and the Talmud. Unusually,
he passed his knowledge on to his daughters. Maimonides, a brilliant polymath and physician to the
sultan of Egypt, is best known for the *Mishneh Torah*,
an attempt to codify Jewish law and make it accessible
to all (see pp.44–5), and *The Guide for the Perplexed*, a

rationalist philosophical defense of the Jewish faith that has had an influence far beyond the confines of Judaism.

Moses Mendelssohn (1729–86) was arguably the first modern Jew. A brilliant scholar and philosopher, he was the darling of the non-Jewish German intelligentsia at a time when Jews were beginning to break through the social barriers that made them second-class citizens. As a driving force behind the Haskalah (the "Jewish Enlightenment"), Mendelssohn sought to meld general European Enlightenment ideals with Judaism and was the first to confront a question that has occupied Judaism ever since: how to retain one's identity as a Jew, yet be open and receptive to modernity.

Theodor Herzl (1860–1904), an Austrian journalist, became convinced that the only solution to the "Jewish question" lay in the Jews again becoming a nation-state. In 1897 he organized the first Zionist Congress, predicting that within fifty years his dream would be realized. Herzl's idea took root and many Jews, particularly those fleeing persecution, joined their coreligionists in Palestine. With the backing of the United Nations, the State of Israel was declared on May 14, 1948. In 1949, the remains of Herzl, the spiritual founder of modern Israel, were brought from Vienna and reburied in Jerusalem.

Maimonides' Thirteen Articles of Faith

66 1. I believe with perfect faith that the Creator, blessed is his name, leads all creatures, and that he by himself made, makes, and will make everything.

2. ... that the Creator ... is unique, and ... that he alone was, is, and will be our God.

3. ... that the Creator ... has no form whatsoever.

4. ... that the Creator ... is the first and is the last.

5. ... that the Creator ... is the only one to whom it is proper to pray....

6. ... that all the words of the prophets are true.

7. ... that the prophecy of Moses our teacher ... was true, and that he was the father of the prophets....

8. ... that the whole of the Torah that is now in our hands was given to Moses our teacher....

9. ... that this Torah will not be exchanged nor will another Torah be given by the Creator....

10. ... that the Creator ... knows all the deeds of humanity and all their thoughts....

11. ... that the Creator ... requites those who keep his commandments with good, but punishes those who transgress his commandments.

12. ... in the coming of the Messiah, and even though he delays ... I will await him ... that he may come.

13. ... that there will be a resurrection of the dead whenever it pleases the Creator ... and his mention is exalted forever and ever. **"**

From "Thirteen Articles of Faith" by Moses Maimonides, translated by Carl S. Ehrlich.

Commentary

Moses Maimonides (1135–1204) was the towering intellectual figure of medieval Jewry. A refugee from Almohad Spain, he settled in Egypt and became a physician to the sultan, a respected rabbi, the most influential Jewish philosopher of all time, and a brilliant codifier of Jewish law, tradition, and beliefs. Sensing that Jewish writings had become too unwieldy for most people to comprehend, Maimonides somewhat immodestly wrote the *Mishneh Torah* ("Second Torah"), in addition to the *Guide for the Perplexed* and the *Sefer ha-Mitzvot* ("Book of Commandments"). In one of his early works, a commentary on the Mishnah, Maimonides distilled a Jewish credo in answer to similar credos among Christians and Muslims. An abbreviated version of his "Thirteen Articles of Faith" is found opposite. Although it engendered controversy in his own time, and is not accepted literally by all Jews today, the credo's great influence on Jewish thought can be seen in the popular hymn *Yigdal* ("May he be magnified"), which is based on it and can be found in the standard Jewish prayerbook.

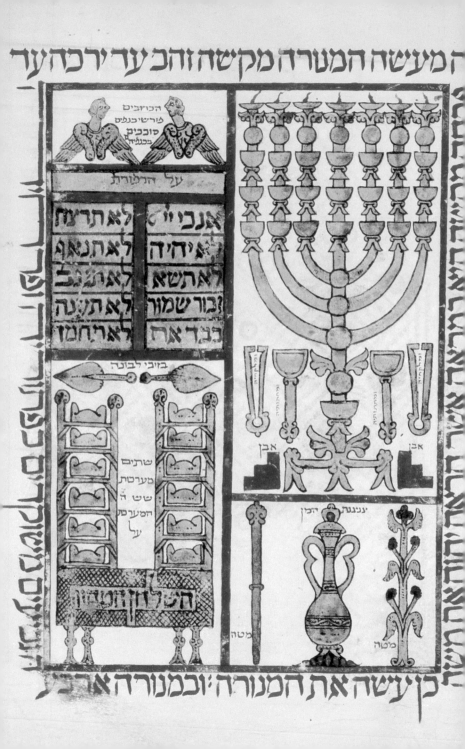

הכרובים
פורשי כנפים
סוככים בכנפיהם

על הכפרת

אנכי יי לא תרצח
אשר יהיה לא תנאף
לא תשא לא תגנב
זכור שמור לא תענה
כבד את לא תחמד

בימי לבונה

שתים
מערכת
שש ה
המערכת
על

השלחן וכליו

אבן   אבן

ענבעת הכן

מטה   מטה

CHAPTER FIVE

ETHICAL PRINCIPLES

The various commandments that regulate a traditional Jewish life are understood as an expression of the devotion of Jews to living an ethical and moral existence in emulation of divine holiness. No rational reason is given for them, other than that they are the demands that God has placed on the Jewish people. Thus, they are inherently good—fulfilling a commandment is viewed as a "good deed" and as an act of sanctification of God's name. Great emphasis is placed upon the betterment of the world as a whole. It is therefore not surprising that Jews have often been at the forefront of movements for social change. While Judaism recognizes that humans are complex creatures, there is the hope that a person will devote him- or herself more fully to doing good, than to doing evil.

LEFT: Title page of the Perpignan Bible, France 1299. It depicts important ritual objects associated with the Temple cult that are mentioned in the Torah, including the menorah (see p.75), the Ten Commandments, the cherubim, incense shovels, Aaron's staff, and a jar with manna.

In Judaism, the belief in one God is intimately tied in with the ethical principles that regulate human life. An ethical life is both a gesture of devotion to God's will and an imitation of the divine. Since God is holy and just, Jews must emulate God in these and all other aspects of the divine being. Forming the basis of an ethical life are the six hundred and thirteen commandments (*mitzvot*) that the rabbis distilled from the Pentateuch or Torah proper (see pp.38–9). These commandments, together with the enormous body of traditions based upon them, are known as the *halakhah*, literally "walk"—that is, the way in which Israel is to walk in this world.

In the Talmud tractate *Pirke Avot* ("Ethics of the Fathers"), the teacher Simon the Just claims that the world is founded upon Torah (the commandments and their performance), divine service (worship and praise of God), and acts of loving-kindness (good deeds toward one's fellow human beings). In the same work, Simon ben Gamliel puts it more abstractly when he claims that the world exists because of truth, justice, and peace. In neither case is the potential reward for ethical behavior the factor that motivates a life of goodness: one does good deeds for their own sake, because they are divinely ordained *mitzvot*. The performance of the *mitzvot*, especially in adversity, is seen as the sanctification of God's name (*kiddush ha-Shem*), while breaching them besmirches it (*hillul ha-Shem*).

Providing for the poor, weak, and disadvantaged thus takes on a religious significance, and the care of others has played a large part in the development of a Jewish ethic. Jewish communities have traditionally had highly organized systems of social welfare, to which all have been required to contribute according to their ability. Another factor is the concept of *tikkun olam* ("betterment of the world"), the desire to leave the world a better place than when one entered it. All these elements help to explain why Jews have often been at the forefront of the struggle for justice and social change in the modern world.

Judaism does not subscribe to the doctrine of original sin, but believes each human being to be born with the potential for doing both good and evil. The individual has to bear the responsibility for his or her actions and life becomes a struggle between the inclination to good (*yetzer ha-tov*) and the inclination to evil (*yetzer ha-ra*). One who struggles with moral ambiguity and triumphs over temptation is—according to one view—more highly regarded than one who has led a completely blameless life. Free will is an important

This scene from the Golden Haggadah *(Spain, 14th century) illustrates the distribution of* matzot *("unleavened breads") to the needy prior to the celebration of Passover (see pp.82–4).*

concept in Judaism. Unlike an animal, a human being is able to choose between right and wrong. Nonetheless, God is omniscient and thus knows which course a person will choose.

Rabbinic theology asserts that any righteous person, Jew or gentile, can attain the world to come. While Jews are expected to live according to the 613 commandments, the ethical system of gentiles must accord with the seven "Noahide laws," which God set for Noah after the legendary Flood. These ban idolatry, blasphemy, murder, sexual crimes, theft, and cruelty to animals; and recommend the building of courts of law.

There are two categories of ethical injunctions in Judaism: those that pertain to the relationship between humanity and God, and those that concern the relationships between human beings. On Yom Kippur, the Day of Repentance, or Atonement, the community confesses its communal transgressions against God who then forgives the community. However, atonement is not complete unless each individual has asked for forgiveness from those people whom he or she may have harmed in the past year. God cannot forgive transgressions that take place between human beings, only those that are directed against God.

The Jewish dietary laws (*kashrut*) are an expression of the sanctity of life. In the Jewish view, since vegetarianism is the ideal state, and the consumption of meat was a concession made by God after the Flood, not all animals can be consumed. Those that can must be killed as quickly and painlessly as possible—a creature that suffers unduly is not *kosher* ("suitable," "fit"). Cruelty to animals in general violates basic Jewish ethical belief, hence Judaism outlaws hunting.

A Letter from the "Genius of Vilnius"

" . . . I also ask my wife to honor my mother as it is written in the Torah, particularly as regards widows. It would be a criminal offence to cause her the slightest distress. And I also ask my mother to ensure that there will be peace between the two of them. Each woman should make the other happy through pleasant words, for this is an important commandment for every human being. After all, every person is asked at the moment of judgment whether he has walked beside his fellow with a calm spirit. In this manner, the Torah lays great stress on making people happy. Let there be no strife among any members of the household, neither male nor female, but let there be love and brotherhood. And should one of you do something that is not acceptable, let them forgive him and live together in peace for God's sake. I have also asked my mother that she teach my sons and daughters with gentle words, so they will accept them. Let her also watch over them. And I command my sons and daughters to honor her. Let there be heard among them no argument or anger at all, but let all be peaceful. May the Master of Peace give them, my sons, my daughters, my sons-in-law, my brothers and all Israel life and peace. **"**

From a letter by the Vilna Gaon, translated by Carl S. Ehrlich.

Commentary

Because the position of the Jews in medieval Europe was precarious, there was no assurance that one generation would inherit anything of monetary value from the previous one. Thus, a genre of literature known as "ethical wills" was born. In lieu of goods, parents would leave their children their accumulated ethical and moral wisdom, which was contained in a formal will.

The excerpt opposite is strictly speaking not an "ethical will," but a letter written by one of the most illustrious Jewish scholars of the pre-modern period—Elijah, son of Solomon Zalman, known as the Vilna Gaon (the "Genius of Vilnius," 1720–1797)—to his family while on a journey. As the leader of the Mitnagdim ("opponents"), the Vilna Gaon was the champion of the Eastern European intellectual orthodoxy against which the Hasidim (see pp.100–102) were rebelling. Owing to his memorization of the gamut of traditional Jewish literature, the Vilna Gaon was the foremost *halakhic* ("legal") expert of his day. But in this letter we see an unexpected side of him, as a family man, not as a fearsome intellect.

In this letter, as in ethical wills, he urges his family to follow the divine ethical teachings. Among the issues stressed are learning, peace, devotion, honesty, and good conduct toward one's fellow human beings.

CHAPTER SIX

SACRED SPACE

There are two main categories of sacred space in Judaism. The first is space that is considered inherently holy— this type of space is centered in the holy land of Israel, which is home not only to the city of Jerusalem, but also to the holiest of all Jewish sites, the Western Wall of the platform supporting the ancient Temples.

The second type of scared space is that which is made holy by virtue of the acts that are performed there. Such space can be subdivided into the public and private spheres. Thus, the synagogue becomes holy as a result of the public actions that take place within it, and the home becomes holy by virtue of what the family does to sanctify its existence. Finally, over the years, a number of other significant sites and symbols have emerged that are strongly identified with the Jewish faith.

LEFT: The interior of the synagogue at Carpentras, the oldest synagogue in France. The lectern upon which the Torah scroll is placed is in the foreground. The Torah shrine, or ark, is in the background. The menorah (see p.10 and p.75) appears as a prominent artistic motif.

Judaism is at the same time community-oriented and family-oriented. In the modern world, this is reflected in two major types of sacred space: the synagogue and the home. In a sense, the precursor to both was the Temple of Jerusalem, the central shrine of Judaism in ancient times, which stood on a vast raised platform (the Temple Mount or Haram esh-Sharif), where the Muslim Dome of the Rock and al-Aqsa mosque stand today. The Bible is the only witness to the First Temple, which was erected by King Solomon and stood from ca. 950–586BCE. It may have begun as a chapel attached to the royal palace, which was the case with a number of similar structures in other Near Eastern cultures.

Solomon's Temple was destroyed by the Babylonians but was rebuilt under the Persians and rededicated in 515BCE. This Second Temple was most likely an unimposing structure until King Herod the Great of Judea (37–4BCE) refurbished it on a grand scale. Its glory was short-lived, because it was destroyed in 70CE by the Romans. Nothing of the Temple itself remains today, although part of the great platform on which it stood, extended by Herod and supported by massive retaining walls, can still be seen. The surviving Herodian masonry includes the Western Wall. The ruins of the destroyed Temple retained their holiness, despite the fact that almost all trace of them was removed by subsequent building activity. For many centuries, Jews were denied access to the Temple Mount variously by the Romans, Christians, and Muslims, and they shifted their devotion to the extant section of the western retaining wall. Certain Jewish religious authorities also declared the Temple Mount off-limits, for fear that someone might tread inadvertently where the Holy of Holies had once stood. The Western, or "Wailing," Wall, a section of the retaining wall of the Temple platform, thus became the holiest site in Judaism.

The original Temple precincts clearly had areas of increasing holiness and more limited access the closer one came to the central sanctuary. In Herodian times, these included the Court of the Gentiles, beyond which non-Jews could not go, then the Court of Women, the Court of the Israelites (that is, male Jews only), and the Court of the Priests. The Temple itself had a forecourt, a main hall, and finally an inner sanctum (the Holy of Holies) to which the high priest alone had access, on one day of the year (Yom Kippur, the Day of Repentance, or Atonement; see p.81). The Temple was neither a democratic nor an egalitarian institution.

According to the Bible, God's blessing for Abraham consisted of a twofold promise of descendants and of land. The Jewish people view themselves as the fulfillment of the first promise; the second is fulfilled by the people of Israel dwelling in the land of Israel. It is perhaps a uniquely Jewish paradox that a religion to which a person born anywhere in the world can belong is yet intimately bound to one small territory.

According to Jewish belief, just as there were levels of holiness in the layout of the Temple, there are also levels of geographical holiness. Israel is referred to as the Holy Land, the capital of which is Jerusalem, the Holy City. It is the navel of the world (Ezekiel 5.5, 38.12), where the divine and the human spheres are in closer contact than anywhere else. The land of Israel is the axis around which all of Jewish life revolves. The Jewish calendar (see p.80), which determines observance throughout the world, is attuned solely to the change of seasons as they occur in Israel. For centuries, the religious life of every Jew was lived in remembrance of the passage of time in a land that was often very far away.

Since the destruction of the First Temple, a sizeable portion of the Jewish people has lived more or less permanently in exile. There were times during which the communities of the Diaspora, living outside the Holy Land, were the leaders in Jewish life, and times during which the Jewish community of Israel was the

Women praying at the Western Wall in Jerusalem. It is traditional to place slips of paper containing requests and petitions in the cracks between the massive stones of the Wall.

most important. The give and take between Israel and the Diaspora has been one of the creative tensions underlying the development of Judaism.

Yet, no matter how established they have been in the lands of their dispersion, or how loyal they may have been to the countries in which they have dwelt, the attachment to the land of Israel and the hope for a restoration to it in the messianic age (see pp.30–3) have played a central role in the identity and theology of Jews the world over. The birth of the modern state of Israel so soon after the Holocaust, and the subsequent integration into the state of Jewish refugees from all over the world, has been reckoned as one of the great miracles of Jewish history. For some, the founding of a Jewish state nearly two millennia after the end of the last one is a harbinger of the messianic age (*athalta d'geulah*).

The origins of the synagogue are uncertain. The Jews must have developed some way of continuing their religious and communal life in exile following the destruction of the First Temple in the sixth century BCE. However, the first archeologically attested synagogues date from about half a millennium later, toward the end of the Second Temple period. The word "synagogue" itself, derived from a Greek rendering of the Hebrew *bet keneset* ("gathering place"), indicates its communal function. Thus, while the Second Temple was still standing, the synagogue already existed as an identifiable and separate institution. After 70CE, with the rise and triumph of rabbinic Judaism, which had its power base in the synagogue, it can be argued that the Temple became superfluous to the continuing existence of Judaism, in spite of never-ending Jewish hopes for its rebuilding.

The loss of the Temple resulted in an expansion of the role of the synagogue from a communal center and house of study to an establishment for religious services previously provided by the Temple. Much of the Temple ritual centered on sacrifices, which in Jewish law could be offered at no other place. In the synagogue, therefore, sacrifices were replaced by further study and communal divine services. This was to have a profound effect on the development of rabbinic Judaism, which tried to keep the memory of the Temple rituals alive in the eventuality that the sanctuary would be restored, but also continued the process of reinterpreting those rituals and establishing the synagogue as an independent entity. Through the institution of the synagogue, rabbinic Judaism brought about the empowerment of the individual Jew. In the Jewish view, this finally led to the realization of the biblical description of Israel as "a priestly kingdom and a holy nation" (Exodus 19.6).

While the Temple and its site are inherently holy for Judaism, it is not a synagogue itself that is sacred, but the actions performed there and the objects deposited within its walls (the Torah scrolls, Judaism's most precious objects, and the prayerbooks; see pp.38–47). These are what make a synagogue the "small sanctuary" (Ezekiel 11.16) of Israel in exile, without a Temple. Synagogues are traditionally oriented toward Jerusalem. On the interior of the wall facing the Holy City is a niche or "ark" housing the Torah scrolls. Prominent in Orthodox synagogues is the separate seating area for women, often located behind a curtain or in a balconied gallery.

With the redefinition and reapplication of Temple ritual in rabbinic Judaism, the Jewish home has also become a place for the sacred. Indicating this is the *mezuzah*, a small box containing a parchment scroll affixed to the doorposts of Jewish homes (see p.35). The *mezuzah* contains the words of the central confession of faith, the Shema prayer (Deuteronomy 6.4) and the first two of its associated blessings. It serves to show that when one crosses the threshold of the home, one is entering a space devoted to God and to a certain code of ethics. Although the rabbis of the talmudic age instituted synagogue worship to correspond to the schedule of sacrifices in the Temple, at home the sacrificial altar has been replaced by the table. In a domestic setting, eating assumes a ritual connotation and becomes for Jews a holy act of divine service of the utmost importance.

A place of holiness to Jews may contain any of a number of significant Jewish symbols. For many, the first that comes to mind is the six-pointed "Star of David" (*Magen David*). Yet this is a relatively modern symbol, having been first employed as such in late medieval Prague. Mosaic synagogue floors from the Roman and Byzantine periods give us a glimpse of what the Jews of the formative rabbinic age viewed as their characteristic symbols. Pride of place belongs to the seven-branched candelabrum (*menorah*), which is also depicted in a famous relief on the Arch of Titus in Rome that shows objects looted from the Temple in 70CE. This is still a clearly recognizable Jewish symbol, as in many quarters is the ram's horn trumpet (*shofar*).

Although Judaism officially eschews personality cults, various sites have been identified as the graves of biblical figures and become objects of pilgrimage. The tombs of famous rabbis and other spiritual leaders have also become sites of veneration, as have places associated with the glories or agonies of Jewish history. The Western Wall (see pp.68–9), remains Judaism's most popular pilgrimage destination.

Longing for the Spiritual Homeland

❝ My heart is in the east, but I am at the farthest reaches
of the west—
How can I taste what I eat; and how can it agree with me?
How can I fulfil my vows or my pledges, while Zion
is in the territory of Edom, and I am chained
to the west?
It would be as easy for me to renounce all the good
of Spain, as
It would be precious for me to see the dust of
the ruined sanctuary. **❞**

My Heart is in the East by Judah Halevi, translated by Carl S. Ehrlich.

❝ ... Even the hero, whose praises we sing,
Even Judah son of Halevi
Had his beloved damsel;
Yet, she was a special type. ...

The one, whom the Rabbi loved,
Was a sad and poor beloved,
The very picture of distress and destruction,
And she was called Jerusalem. .... **❞**

From *Jehuda ben Halevy* by Heinrich Heine, translated by Carl S. Ehrlich.

Commentary

Judah Halevi (ca. 1075–ca. 1141) was one of the most important figures of the end of the "Golden Age" in Spain. Among his many works were about eight hundred poems, which range from erotic love poetry to laments. The poem opposite is his most famous. From his years of wandering in Spain between the Christian and Muslim worlds, Halevi came to the conclusion that a true Jewish life could only be lived in the land of Israel, or Zion. "My Heart Is in the East" expresses the poet's longing for the ancient homeland. Eventually, he set out for the Holy Land, but appears to have died on the way in Egypt. According to legend, he reached Israel, only to be murdered by a marauding soldier.

Heinrich Heine (1797–1856) was a brilliant poet and satirist who straddled Jewish and Christian society in the first half of the nineteenth century. Although he opportunistically converted to Christianity in his twenties, he never forgot his Jewish roots and published frequently on Jewish themes, particularly during his final years, when he claimed that his conversion was a sham. Among his sympathetic portraits of Judaism is his poem about Halevi (see extract, opposite), in which Halevi's attachment to Zion comes to the fore and the legend of his death in the Holy Land is repeated.

CHAPTER SEVEN

SACRED TIME

A traditional Jewish life is structured to express both ethical and religious concerns and a sense of connectedness to Jewish historical experience. Rituals are attuned to daily, weekly, monthly, and yearly cycles, as well as to the rhythm of key lifecycle events. In theory, the most important day of the Jewish calendar is the Sabbath, although in practice, holidays that come but once a year are given precedence.

Jewish holiday observance is based on the annual agricultural cycle of the land of Israel, fostering an attachment to the rhythms of life in the ancient homeland, even if one lives far away from it. Time-based ceremonies also serve a didactic purpose in reliving the many highs and lows of Jewish history. Lifecycle rituals provide a link to the generations that have come before and that will come in the future.

LEFT: A man wearing a prayer shawl blows a shofar *("ram's horn").* The shofar *is blown on Rosh Hashanah (New Year) and again at the conclusion of Yom Kippur (Day of Atonement).*

The individual's relationship with God and thankfulness for the gift of life are predominant in daily ritual. In addition to the three times a day that Jews are supposed to pray, there are blessings for almost any situation that arises in the course of a day, thereby embuing even the most mundane of tasks with holiness.

The scholar Ahad Ha-Am (1856–1927) said: "More than Israel has kept the Sabbath, the Sabbath has kept Israel." The observance of a universal day of prayer, study, and rest every seventh day has served to bind the Jewish people since ancient times. The Sabbath (Hebrew, *Shabbat*) lasts from sundown on Friday until nightfall on Saturday. Candles are lit at both the beginning and end of the Sabbath to mark the division between the mundane workweek and the holy suspension of worldly time. Since it is a day of rest, one should not work on the Sabbath.

The ancient Jewish calendar is still used in a religious context. Its starting point is the Creation, as calculated from the Bible: thus 2003CE corresponds to the Jewish year 5763–64. The annual calendar combines solar and lunar reckoning. Months are calculated according to the phases of the moon. Nevertheless, seven times in every nineteen-year cycle, a leap-month is added so that holidays continue to fall in the correct season.

Although the first month of the Jewish calendar falls in the spring, the Jewish New Year (Rosh Hashanah) is not celebrated until the seventh month (Tishri, September/October). Rosh Hashanah celebrates the annual renewal of God's creative act at the moment the agricultural cycle comes full circle. The New Year ushers in a ten-day period of reflection known as the "Days of Awe" (Yamim Noraim). The climax of this period is Yom Kippur (Day of Repentance, or Atonement), which is a strict fast day devoted to communal repentance before God. It is traditional to dress in white and to abstain from various activities, such as bathing and sex.

Five days later begins the weeklong celebration of Sukkot (the Feast of Tabernacles), the first of the three annual "pilgrimage festivals" (so called because in ancient times Jewish men were called upon to visit the Temple in Jerusalem on these occasions). Originally a commemoration of the end of the harvest season, it has been given an added significance in Judaism. The temporary shelters or booths (*sukkot*, singular *sukkah*) inhabited by the ancient farmers during the harvest season have been reinterpreted to represent the dwellings of the Israelites during their forty years of wandering in the desert before reaching the promised land. During Sukkot it is traditional to eat or to sleep in these booths.

A family of Yemenite immigrants celebrates the Passover Seder in Israel. The table is set with symbolic foods, and the head of the household raises a piece of matzah *("unleavened bread").*

At the end of Sukkot comes the double holiday of Shemini Atzeret ("Eighth Day of Assembly"), a biblical observance of uncertain significance, and Simhat Torah ("Rejoicing in the Torah"), a joyous holiday on which the annual cycle of weekly Torah readings is completed and recommenced with the celebratory reading of Deuteronomy 34 and Genesis 1.

The eight-day midwinter festival of Hanukkah, or Chanukah ("Rededication"), commemorates the rededication in 164BCE of the Temple in Jerusalem (see p.14). According to a later legend, the holiday celebrates the miracle of a measure of oil that burned for eight days instead of the one day expected.

The Fifteenth Day of Shvat (Tu Bishvat, January/February) marks the season for planting trees in the land of Israel. Outside Israel, Jews plant trees as the weather permits. A feature of the modern festival is fundraising for reforestation projects in Israel.

The popular holiday of Purim commemorates the rescue of the Jews from an impending massacre in the days of the Persian empire, as recounted in the Book of Esther, the communal reading of which forms the centerpiece of the festival. Purim, a lesson of hope for generations of Jews, has assumed a carnival-like atmosphere, with parades and costumes. The giving of presents, in particular to the poor, is also a feature of Purim.

The weeklong observance of Passover (Pesach) begins in the first month (March/April). Originally a pilgrimage festival celebrating the first fruits of the agricultural year, Passover has been remodelled as a commemoration of the Exodus from Egypt. The major component is a lavish ritual meal (Seder) at which the story of the Exodus is recounted from the Haggadah (see pp.46–7). Young and old are required to view themselves as personally freed from bondage.

Seven weeks after the beginning of Pesach falls the third of the pilgrimage festivals, Shavuot (the Feast of Weeks, or Pentecost), originally a commemoration of the wheat harvest. It celebrates the revelation on Mount Sinai seven weeks after the Exodus.

The Ninth Day of Av (Tishah b'Av), in July or August, is a postbiblical fast day on which a number of disasters in Jewish history are said to have occurred, such as the destruction of the Temple in 586BCE and 70CE, and the expulsion of the Jews from Spain in 1492.

Two modern holidays have become popular. Holocaust Remembrance Day (Yom ha-Shoah) is observed in memory of the six million Jews murdered by the Nazis and their allies in the Second World War. By contrast, Israel Independence Day (Yom ha-Atzmaut) is a joyful celebration of the seemingly miraculous regeneration of the Jewish people after the depths of the Holocaust.

In Judaism, great emphasis is placed on key stages of the individual's lifecycle. From birth to death, there is a ritual for everything (for death rituals, see pp.91–5).

At the age of eight days, a male child enters into the Jewish community, and partakes of its covenant with

God, by virtue of his ritual circumcision (*brit milah*, "covenant of circumcision"), during which he receives his name. A girl is traditionally welcomed into the Jewish people and given her name at a Sabbath service, but in recent times, liberal Jews have developed ceremonies for celebrating the birth of a daughter that are intended to be more analogous to the *brit milah*.

A boy's attainment of religious maturity has been celebrated in the *bar mitzvah* ("son of the commandment") ceremony, at which the thirteen-year-old is called up to read from the Torah for the first time. Liberal Jews also accord this honor to girls in the equivalent ceremony of *bat mitzvah* ("daughter of the commandment").

A marriage ceremony has three main parts. First is the signing of a marriage contract (*ketubbah*), traditionally written in Aramaic. Second is the ring ceremony, or *huppah*, which takes its name from the portable marriage canopy used in the ceremony. The *huppah* is often, but not necessarily, held in the synagogue. The last stage is *yihud*, when the couple are left alone—traditionally to consummate the marriage, although today it is more often a time for a break in the course of a hectic day. The importance of marriage in Judaism is indicated by the prayer in which one wishes that one's children will grow up to a life of "Torah, marriage, and good deeds."

The Diversity of Time

❝ Judaism is a *religion of time* aiming at the *sanctification of time*. Unlike the space-minded man to whom time is unvaried, iterative, homogeneous, to whom all hours are alike, qualitiless, empty shells, the Bible senses the diversified character of time. There are no two hours alike. Every hour is unique and the only one given at the moment, elusive and endlessly precious.

Judaism teaches us to be attached to *holiness in time*, to be attached to sacred events, to learn how to consecrate sanctuaries that emerge from the magnificent stream of a year. The Sabbaths are our great cathedrals; and our Holy of Holies is a shrine that neither the Romans nor the Germans were able to burn; a shrine that even apostasy cannot easily obliterate: the Day of Atonement. According to the ancient rabbis, it is not the observance of the Day of Atonement, but the Day itself, the "essence of the Day," which, with man's repentance, atones for the sins of man.

Jewish ritual may be characterized as the art of significant forms in time, as *architecture of time*. Most of its observances—the Sabbath, the New Moon, the festivals, the Sabbatical and Jubilee year—depend on a certain hour of the day or season of the year. It is, for example, the

evening, morning, or afternoon that brings with it the
call to prayer. The main themes of faith lie in the realm
of time. We remember the day of the exodus from Egypt,
the day when Israel stood at Sinai; and our Messianic
hope is the expectation of a day, of the end of days. **"**

From *The Sabbath: Its Meaning for Modern Man* by Abraham Joshua Heschel New York: Farrar, Straus and
Giroux, 1951, p.8.

Commentary

Polish-born Rabbi Abraham Joshua Heschel (1907–1972)
was one of the most important and influential Jewish
theologians of the twentieth century. Although personally
observant, he criticized those who placed undue emphasis on the letter of the law, while ignoring the spirit that
animated that law.

For Heschel, who marched with Dr. Martin Luther
King at Selma, Judaism is a prophetic religion of morality and ethics. Inspired by the mystical tradition, he
argued that God could indeed be found everywhere in
this world. His God is a compassionate one, who deeply
cares about and constantly searches for the truly human.

This excerpt from his work evidences the depth
of poetic language that Heschel was able to apply to
theological issues—in this case, his discussion about the
Jewish understanding of time, in which time itself
becomes the means for expressing holiness.

CHAPTER EIGHT

DEATH AND THE AFTERLIFE

Although Judaism places its greatest emphasis on what one does and what happens in this world, there has developed a general belief in an afterlife. The great medieval philosopher Maimonides (see pp.56–7) formulated belief in resurrection as one of his "Thirteen Articles of Faith"—despite this, Judaism remains vague about what exactly will happen after death. On the practical side, however, the tradition has developed very precise rituals to deal with death and mourning. Prior to burial, the body is treated with the greatest respect, washed, and enveloped in shrouds. Burial itself takes place as quickly as possible, and is a simple and dignified affair. The rituals surrounding death take special note of the bereaved, who are given an outlet for their grief and then eased back into normal life in a gradual manner.

LEFT: A tomb in the Jewish cemetery on the Mount of Olives, Jerusalem. It is traditional to place stones or pebbles on Jewish tombs, but the exact reason for this custom is unknown. In addition, some Jews place written petitions on the tombs of people viewed as particularly holy.

The focus of Jewish life and thought is very much grounded in the reality of human existence as experienced in this world, as opposed to a world beyond. Nonetheless, there is some evidence of speculation on, and belief in, a life after death.

One of the issues that divided the Jewish sects of Sadducees and Pharisees in the late Second Temple period was that of the belief in a resurrection of the dead. The Sadducees, who comprised the upper priestly class and were quite satisfied with their lot in the world, had no reason whatsoever to speculate on a world-to-come, since they were enjoying all the fruits of this one. The Pharisees, on the other hand, represented the under-class of society. Their lot in life was not particularly pleasant. Hence it is understandable that their hope for a just reward focussed less on this world than on the world-to-come, in which they would finally reap their deserved recompense.

Since rabbinic Judaism, the progenitor of all modern forms of the religion, was itself descended from the Pharisees, belief in an afterlife has become part of Jewish theology. Even so, such belief has never assumed a central role. The rabbis did have a vague notion of a "future world" (*olam ha-ba*) or a "world of truth" (*olam ha-emet*), which followed this earthly existence. However, it was left to popular expressions of Judaism to fill in the often contradictory details. The influential medieval philosopher Maimonides (see pp.56–7) did formulate belief in an afterlife as one of his "Thirteen Articles of Faith"—despite this, he did not define exactly what he understood by it. Although the traditional version of the Amidah prayer, which is recited daily, praises God as the one who "quickens the dead," this can be understood either literally, as indicating that God will resurrect the dead, or figuratively, as evidencing God's omnipotence even over death.

In spite of Judaism's reluctance to formulate a clear notion of life after death, it has developed meticulous guidelines and rituals for dealing with death. These can be classified under two overarching rubrics: as they pertain to the deceased, and as they pertain to the survivors.

As the end approaches, Jews are encouraged to confess their sins before the Great Judge. This indicates a belief in a continuing existence, at least of the soul, in which making an honest reckoning with one's past can only be beneficial. Following the lead of Rabbi Akiva (d. ca. 135CE), who was martyred and died reciting the Shema prayer, it is desirable to die uttering the Shema, Judaism's central confession of faith (see pp.34–5).

Once a person has died, the body is treated with great reverence. The body is prepared for burial by being washed and placed in a white shroud, symbolizing purity and humility. Jewish burial is a simple and swift affair. Because all people who stand before God are alike, ostentation plays no role in the ceremony ("Naked was I when I came forth from my mother's womb, and naked shall I return there." Job 1.21a). Since the dead no longer have a part to play in this world, it is considered impolite to leave the body unburied. Therefore, burial traditionally takes place within a day of death, or as soon as circumstances will allow. A plain coffin is generally used—this permits the body to become one with the earth from whence it came (according to Genesis 3.19) as quickly as possible. It is considered a *mitzvah* ("good deed") to participate in the shovelling of earth over the coffin. Because humanity is created in the image of God and is destined to return to the earth, Judaism frowns upon cremation.

The rituals surrounding the survivors are designed to bring them comfort and to ease them back into normal life. As a sign of mourning, the mourners tear their clothes, often in a symbolic manner. A week of intense grieving, known as *shivah* ("seven" days), follows the funeral—during this time, the mourners refrain from normal activity and stay at home. It is a communal

An anonymous 18th-century painting of a Jewish funeral in Italy. The body is wrapped in simple shrouds and placed in a plain wooden coffin.

responsibility to visit and provide for them, particularly at the times for daily prayer. The bereaved are then eased back into normal life during a month (*sheloshim*, "thirty" days) of somewhat less intense mourning. The transition is complete after another ten months in mourning. The deceased is remembered on the anniversary of his or her death (*yahrzeit*). At all of these times, the traditional prayer of those in mourning, the Kaddish ("Sanctification"), in praise of God, is recited.

The Mourner's Kaddish

❝ May his great name be magnified and sanctified in
the world that he has created according to his good
will; may his kingdom be acknowledged in your
lifetime and in your days, and in the lives of the
whole house of Israel, swiftly and soon, and say:
Amen.

May his great name be blessed forever and ever.

May his holy name, blessed be he, be blessed and
praised, glorified and exalted, raised and lauded,
elevated and credited, above and beyond all blessings
and songs, praises and consolations, which they recite
in the world, and say: Amen.

Let there be enduring peace from heaven, and life, for
us and for all Israel, and say: Amen.

The one who creates peace in his celestial realm will
make peace for us and for all Israel, and say: Amen. **❞**

"The Mourner's Kaddish", translated by Carl S. Ehrlich.

Commentary

The Kaddish ("Sanctification") Prayer, written mainly in
Aramaic, is one of the oldest and most important prayers
in the Jewish liturgy. As a communal prayer, it may only
be recited when there is a quorum (Hebrew, *minyan*)

present, traditionally consisting of ten males who have reached the age of religious maturity (thirteen).

The Kaddish is a doxology, a prayer praising and extolling God. It is antiphonal in nature, with the leader reciting it, and the congregation responding with "blessed be he" and "amen," as appropriate, in addition to "May his great name be blessed for ever and ever."

The Kaddish translated here is the "Mourner's Kaddish" (Hebrew, *Kaddish Yatom*, literally the "Orphan's Kaddish"). The custom of having mourners recite the Kaddish arose in thirteenth-century Germany as a response to persecution by the Crusaders. It is perhaps a strange choice to have this prayer recited by mourners, since it mentions neither the deceased nor the sorrow of the bereaved. On the contrary, it is a public affirmation of God's greatness. At the very moment one may be feeling intense bitterness toward the Deity on account of the death of a loved one, tradition demands that the mourner affirm God and return to life.

The Mourner's Kaddish is to be recited by the bereaved for eleven months following the funeral. After the conclusion of the period of mourning, the bereaved remember the deceased annually on the anniversary (Yiddish, *yahrzeit*) of their death by reciting the Kaddish and lighting a memorial candle.

CHAPTER NINE

SOCIETY AND RELIGION

The Jewish confrontation with modernity has given rise to a number of distinct religious movements within Judaism. The Reform movement, the oldest of the three major movements, views ancient laws and customs as human responses to the divine and, hence, non-binding in nature—it emphasizes the spirit rather than the letter of the law. Neo-Orthodoxy arose as a traditional response to the often radical innovations of the early reformers. Orthodoxy has reaffirmed the divine and binding nature of both the written and the oral Torah. The Conservative movement came into being as an attempt to steer a middle course between Reform and Orthodoxy. Like Orthodoxy, it views both the written and oral Torah as divinely inspired, but is more receptive to change—as is evident in the status of women in Judaism.

LEFT: Since its founding in 1948, the State of Israel has provided a haven for Jews fleeing persecution from throughout the world. Here, a group of Ethiopian Jews (also known as Beta Israel or, pejoratively, as Falashas) celebrates its annual Seged holiday.

For Judaism, the modern period began in the late eighteenth century with the gradual emancipation of the Jews in Western Europe and the Americas from their second-class status. As long as Jews were excluded from society, they were able to retain their distinctive religion and identity. However, in their rush to become fully accepted members of the body politic, many chose the option of Christian baptism. Although the need to convert no longer exists, the temptation to assimilate into liberal Western society continues to exert a strong influence on many Jews. Nonetheless, a great number of other Jews have attempted to come to grips with modernity within the context of Judaism. Their diverse responses have led both to a vibrant renewal of Jewish theology and to deep religious and ideological splits within the larger Jewish community.

The first modern Jewish movement, Reform Judaism, came into being in early nineteenth-century Germany as an attempt to wed Jewish ethical monotheism with the philosophies of post-Enlightenment Europe. It is an eclectic theology, allowing its adherents to choose which aspects of Jewish tradition to follow. It places greater emphasis on ethics than on ritual, and emphasizes social action both within and without the confines of the Jewish community. The Reform movement has had a major influence on other branches of Judaism, and has been to the fore in developing strategies to cope with new social realities. However, since many of the decisions of the Reform movement are reached independently of the other branches of Judaism, it often comes into conflict with its coreligionists.

Of all the Jewish movements, Orthodoxy is the most difficult to define, because it is divided into many different currents, from the centrist modern Orthodox to the Hasidim and ultra-Orthodox on the extreme right. Also, in contrast to other branches of Judaism, it lacks a central organizing body. Modern Orthodoxy was born in mid nineteenth-century Germany as a reaction to the development of radical reformist tendencies. Under the leadership of Rabbi Samson Raphael Hirsch (1808–88), it developed according to the motto "Torah combined with secular knowledge." Like the reformers, Hirsch realized that the Jewish community had to come to grips with modernity. However, Hirsch believed that this could be achieved within the context of a traditionally observant Jewish life. Thus, modern Orthodoxy is open to the scientific investigation of all fields of human knowledge, with the exception of those areas, such as modern biblical criticism, which come into conflict with its basic religious dogmas. A fundamental belief of

Orthodoxy is the divine origin of both the written and the oral Torah, so while new circumstances call for new rulings, the circumstances are interpreted within the context of the *halakhah* (the entire body of Jewish law; see page 60); the *halakhah* is not tailored to fit the circumstances.

For most of the history of rabbinic and postrabbinic Judaism, the authority and divine origin of the *halakhah* went unquestioned. However, rationalism and historicism led to a recognition among those open to these streams of thought that *halakhah* had always been an adaptable system. The divisions among modern Jews have at their root the question of the authority of *halakhah* and whether it is to be viewed as binding in its totality, or as a source of practice from which one can then choose on the basis of an informed personal judgment. According to the latter view, *halakhah* can have a vote, but no veto, on change in practice.

A distinct offshoot of Orthodoxy is Hasidism. Originally a mystical and ecstatic movement, Hasidism began as a reaction against the established orthodoxy of eastern European Judaism. It traces its origins to the teachings of the charismatic Israel ben Eleazar (1700–60), known as the Baal Shem Tov ("Master of the Good Name"). He and his followers tried to rediscover

A girl recites the Haftarah *(a reading from the Prophets) on the occasion of her becoming a* bat mitzvah *("daughter of the commandment"), at the age of either 12 or 13.*

the joy inherent in simple acts of divine service and prayer. They were opposed by the entrenched intellectual orthodoxy of Elijah ben Solomon (1720–97), known as the Vilna Gaon ("Genius of Vilnius," Lithuania; see pp.64–5). Elijah excommunicated the Hasidim—ironically, because Hasidism has evolved into a champion of fundamentalist Orthodoxy in Judaism. The descendants of both groups are now Orthodox allies in the battle against the supposed dilution of traditional Judaism.

The Conservative movement in Judaism came into being as an attempt to find a middle ground between the reformers and the Orthodox. Thus it is "conservative" compared to Reform, but "liberal" in comparison to Orthodox Judaism. Although its intellectual antecedents can also be traced to Germany, the Conservative movement was born in the US. It represented a compromise between the liberal German Jewish reformers, who constituted the majority of nineteenth-century American Jewry, and the traditionally raised eastern European Jewish immigrants who poured into America between 1881 and 1924. Like Orthodoxy, it is based on the *halakhah*, but is more flexible in its interpretation of Jewish tradition—it has, for example, accorded women equality in religious life (as has the Reform movement). The Reconstructionist movement, which views Judaism as a civilization that is constantly evolving, is a small, but influential, offshoot of Conservative Judaism.

While the tragic events of the Holocaust and the creation of the state of Israel served to unite world Jewry for close to half a century, in recent years, Jews have begun to turn part of their attention to internal religious issues. Because of the centrality of Israel to the Jewish people, the modern secular state has often served as the battleground between conflicting denominations. The founders of the Israeli state were for the most part secular Zionists, who were content to leave control of religious and consequent social issues to the official Orthodox authorities. This has led to the division of Israeli society into a religiously disinterested secular majority and a politically powerful Orthodox minority. In order to safeguard their influence, the religious authorities have taken steps to assure the recognition of Orthodoxy as the sole legitimate form of Judaism in Israel. Orthodox Judaism has thus become Israel's state religion, leading to a delegitimation of the other branches of Judaism. Conservative, Reconstructionist, Reform, and "modern Orthodox" Jews the world over have fought back in an attempt to protect the rights of all Jews in Israel, and also to diversify and enrich the sometimes one-dimensional Jewish life in Israel.

Contemporary inner-Jewish turmoil, including tensions between Israel and the communities of the Diaspora, may be frustrating to those who are actively involved in those battles. But they are also a sign of the continued health and vitality of Judaism as a whole.

WOMEN AND JUDAISM

66 May the life of this child be one of happiness, goodness, and wisdom.

May she always seek peace and pursue an end to strife among her fellow human beings.

May she be a shining light to all who know her and may she courageously do what must be done.

Strengthen us to raise our daughter in the path of our Torah and Mitzvot.

Help us to lead her in the footsteps of Sarah, Rebecca, Rachel, and Leah, Miriam, Deborah, Hulda, and Esther.

In the footsteps of all our foremothers and forefathers whose deeds continue to shine across the generations of our people.

Then shall our daughter bring blessing to her family, her people, and the world. **99**

Parental Blessing, from "Simhat Bat," by Rabbi Nina Beth Cardin.

Commentary

Historically, Judaism has developed along patriarchal lines. For the most part, it was men who assumed public roles and determined the interpretation of religious texts and traditions, while women ran the household and, in the first instance, transmitted Judaism to their children.

The rabbis interpreted this situation positively to mean that women were free from time-bound religious obligations (*mitzvot*). Thus, since only men were obliged to engage in daily public prayer, this became their domain and women were exempted (or excluded, depending on one's point of view).

Since the advent of liberal Judaism, women have gained a greater role in Jewish public life. The Reform movement has led the way in redefining the place of women in the synagogue. Mixed rather than single-sex seating in liberal congregations was eventually followed by the equal participation of women in services; and in 1972, Reform Judaism was the first to ordain women rabbis and cantors. This empowerment has also had a considerable influence on Orthodoxy, where the importance of women's Torah study is now acknowledged, and more attention is paid to issues of Jewish law and practice that are of direct concern to women.

The excerpt opposite is an example of a ritual developed in response to Jewish feminist concerns. New rituals are being developed to acknowledge stages in life that specifically affect women—in this case, the birth of a daughter (*simhat bat* "rejoicing in a daughter") is welcomed in a manner equal in importance to that of a son at his circumcision (*brit milah*).

GLOSSARY

Ashkenazim Jews descended from the medieval communities of Germany (they form the majority in North America and northern and eastern Europe).

Conservative Judaism centrist movement in modern Judaism; conservative in respect to Reform, but liberal in respect to Orthodoxy.

Diaspora general designation for Jewish communities outside the land of Israel.

Hasidism an ecstatic movement that arose in pre-modern Eastern Europe.

Holocaust – the systematic attempt to exterminate European Jewry during World War II.

Kabbalah the dominant mystical tradition in medieval Judaism.

Kaddish a prayer sanctifying God, a version of which is recited by those in mourning.

Kashrut the Jewish dietary laws, which regulate keeping *kosher*.

Maimonides the greatest scholar of medieval Judaism.

menorah the seven-branched candelabrum that is Judaism's oldest symbol.

midrash, **Midrash** both the method of Jewish interpretation of sacred texts and a term for the literature derived from it.

mitzvah commandment and – by extension – a good deed.

Moses the foundational figure of Judaism and archetypal Jew, who led the Israelites out of slavery in Egypt and gave them the Torah.

Orthodoxy the traditional wing of modern Judaism.

Reform Judaism the most liberal of the major modern Jewish movements, it arose in early nineteenth-century Germany.

Rosh Hashanah the Jewish New Year, it takes place in September/October.

Seder the ritual meal associated with the holiday of Passover (Pesach), commemorating the Exodus from Egypt.

Sephardim Jews descended from the medieval community of Spain.

Shema the central Jewish declaration of faith in one God.

Talmud the major theological and practical work of post-biblical Judaism.

Tanakh acronym for the Hebrew Bible, consisting of the Torah (Pentateuch), Nevi'im (Prophets), and Ketuvim (Writings).

Torah the first five books of the Bible and Judaism's central text.

YHWH the Tetragrammaton, the ineffable four-letter name of God.

GENERAL BIBLIOGRAPHY

Avineri, Shlomo. *The Making of Modern Zionism: The Intellectual Origins of the Jewish State*. New York: Basic Books, 1981.

Biale, David, ed. *Cultures of the Jews: A New History*. New York: Schocken Books, 2002.

Bialik, Hayim Nachman, and Yehoshua Hana Ravnitzky, eds. *The Book of Legends (Sefer Ha-Aggadah): Legends from the Talmud and Midrash*. (William G. Braude, trans.) New York: Schocken Books, 1992.

Cohen, Arthur A., and Paul Mendes-Flohr, eds. *Contemporary Jewish Religious Thought: Original Essays on Critical Concepts, Movements, and Beliefs*. New York: The Free Press and London: Collier Macmillan Publishers, 1987.

Ehrlich, Carl S. "Moses, Torah, and Judaism" in D.N. Freedman and M.J. McClymond, eds. *The Rivers of Paradise: Moses, Buddha, Confucius, Jesus, and Muhammad as Religious Founders*. Grand Rapids, Michigan: Eerdmans, 2001, pp.11–119.

Elbogen, Ismar. *Jewish Liturgy: A Comprehensive History*. (Raymond P. Scheindlin, trans.) Philadelphia: Jewish Publication Society, and New York and Jerusalem: Jewish Theological Seminary of America, 1993

Gillman, Neil. *The Death of Death: Resurrection and Immortality in Jewish Thought*. Woodstock, Vermont: Jewish Lights Publishing, 1997.

Gradenwitz, Peter. *The Music of Israel: From the Biblical Era to Modern Times*. 2nd ed. Portland, Oregon: Amadeus Press, 1996.

Green, Arthur, ed. *Jewish Spirituality*. 2 Vols. New York: Crossroad, 1987.

Grossman, Grace Cohen. *Jewish Art*. Hugh Lauter Levin Associates, 1995

Holtz, Barry W., ed. *Back to the Sources: Reading the Classic Jewish Sources*. New York: Summit Books, 1984.

de Lange, Nicholas, ed. *The Illustrated History of the Jewish People*. Toronto: Key Porter Books, 1997.

Mendes-Flohr, Paul, and Jehuda Reinharz, eds. *The Jew in the Modern World: A Documentary History*. New York: Oxford University Press, 1980.

Plaskow, Judith. *Standing Again at Sinai: Judaism from a Feminist Perspective*. San Francisco: Harper & Row, 1990.

Roth, Cecil, ed. *Encyclopaedia Judaica*. 16 Vols. Jerusalem: Keter Publishing, 1972.

Strassfeld, Michael. *The Jewish Holidays: A Guide and Commentary*. New York-Grand Rapids-Philadelphia-St. Louis-San Francisco-London-Singapore-Sydney-Tokyo-Toronto: Harper & Row, 1985.

Tanakh: A New Translation of the Holy Scriptures According to the Traditional Hebrew Text. Philadelphia: Jewish Publication Society, 1985.

Telushkin, Joseph. *Jewish Literacy: The Most Important Things to Know about the Jewish Religion, Its People, and Its History*. New York: William Morrow and Company, 1991.

INDEX

Page numbers in **bold** refer to major references: page numbers in *italics* refer to captions.

ACKNOWLEDGMENTS AND PICTURE CREDITS

Unless cited otherwise here, text extracts are out of copyright or the product of the author's own translation. The following sources have kindly given their permission.

Sacred Time, p.86: from *The Sabbath: Its Meaning for Modern Man* by Abraham Joshua Heschel. Farrar, Straus and Giroux: New York, 1951, p.8.

Society and Religion, p.104: A parental blessing from "Simhat Bat" by Rabbi Nina Beth Cardin, courtesy ritualwell.org.

The publisher would like to thank the following people, museums, and photographic libraries for permission to reproduce their material. Every care has been taken to trace copyright holders. However, if we have omitted anyone we apologize, and will, if informed, make corrections in any future edition. **Page 2** Corbis/ Annie Griffiths Belt; **8** British Museum, London; **10** AKG London/British Library, London; **12** Corbis/Shai Ginott; **20** AKG London/University Library, Heidelberg; **24** AKG London/ Skirball Museum, Los Angeles/ Erich Lessing; **28** British Library, London; **36** AKG London/ Erich Lessing; **40** Corbis/ Christies; **50** Corbis/Peter M Wilson; **54** AKG London/Judaica-Collection Max Berger, Vienna/Erich Lessing; **58** AKG London/Bibliothèque Nationale, Paris; **62** British Library, London; **66** Corbis/Gail Mooney; **70** Getty/Stone ; **78** Corbis/Ted Spiegel; **82** Corbis/Stock Market/ Richard Nowitz; **88** Magnum/ Fred Mayer; **93** AKG London/ Israel Museum, Jerusalem/Erich Lessing; **96** Corbis Saba/Ricki Rosen; **101** Corbis/Stock Market/ Richard Nowitz